Januar

What's your ideal way to spend a vacation?

Year:: ---------------------------

January 2

What makes you dislike a person?

Year: ------------------------------

January 3

Do you think you are a confident person?
Why or why not?

Year: ---------------------------------

January 4

What about yourself are you most proud of?

Year:: -------------------------------

_____

_____

_____

_____

_____

_____

_____

_____

January 5

What would the best version of you be like?

Year: ----------------------------

_____

_____

_____

_____

_____

_____

_____

_____

January 6

What life experiences did you miss out on?

Year: ---------------------------------

January 7

When are you the most "you"?

Year:: ----------------------------

January 8

How did you fall out with
some of your previously
close friends?

Year: ----------------------------

January 9

Are you happy with the people
you surround yourself with?
Why or why not?

Year:: -------------------------------

January 10

What musical instrument do
you wish you could play?

Year:: ------------------------------

January 11

When has a mundane
occurrence or chance
completely changed the course
of your life?

Year: -----------------------------

January 12

What is the nicest compliment you've received?

Year: ------------------------------

January 13

What age would you like to live to?

Year:: ----------------------------

January 14

If you could travel to any country in the world for one month, where would you go?

Year: ------------------------------

January 15

What is your favorite memory of someone who isn't in your life anymore?

Year:: ----------------------------

January 16

How superstitious are you?

Year:: --------------------------------

January 17

What has been a recurring
theme in your life?

Year: ----------------------------

January 18

What was your most inappropriate or embarrassing fart?

Year:: ----------------------------

_____

_____

_____

_____

_____

_____

_____

_____

January 19

What do you think happens after death?

Year: _____

_____

_____

_____

_____

_____

_____

_____

January 20

What are your top 5 rules for life?

Year: -------------------------------

_____

_____

_____

_____

_____

_____

_____

_____

January 21

What's your favorite thing in your / our house?

Year::

January 22

What book or movie do you wish you could experience for the first time again?

Year: -------------------------

January 23

If you had a friend who spoke to you the same way you speak to yourself, would you keep them as a friend?

Year: ------------------------------

January 24

What petty thing that people do really gets on your nerves?

Year: ------------------------------

January 25

What brings meaning to your life?

Year: _____

_____

_____

_____

_____

_____

_____

_____

January 26

What is something you wish you could say to people but can't?

Year: ------------------------------

January 27

What are some of the most attractive traits a person can have?

Year:: --------------------------------

January 28

What's a secret you've never told anyone?

Year: ------------------------

January 29

What small pleasures do you enjoy the most?

Year: ----------------------------------

_____

_____

_____

_____

_____

_____

_____

_____

January 30

Who is the most irritating person you know?

Year: ----------------------------

January 31

What has been your biggest screw up so far?

Year: ------------------------------

February 1

What have you struggled
with your entire life?

Year: -------------------------

February 2

What is the most significant change you would like to make in your life?

Year:: ---------------------------------

February 3

What do you want out of life?

Year: ------------------------------

February 4

What calms you down the most?

Year: ----------------------------

February 5

What are kinds of things do
you find repulsive?

Year: -----------------------------

February 6

What would your perfect life look like?

Year:: ------------------------------

February 7

If you received a salary to follow whatever passion you wanted to, what would you do?

Year: ------------------------------

February 8

What's your most embarrassing story about being sick?

Year:: -------------------------------

February 9

What friend have you not
thought about in a long time?

Year:: ----------------------------

February 10

What's the craziest thing that has happened at a job you worked at?

Year: --------------------------------

February 11

Who do you act nice around but secretly dislike?

Year: ----------------------------

February 12

If money was no object, and with no input from me, how would you decorate your / our house?

Year:: -----------------------------

February 13

What's your ideal way to
spend a vacation?

Year: -----------------------------

February 14

How good are you at reading people?

Year:: -------------------------------

February 15

Are you hopeful about your future?

Year:: --------------------------

February 16

Who do you want to be more like or who do you look up to most?

Year: --------------------------------

February 17

What were the healthiest and unhealthiest periods of your life?

Year: --

February 18

What's the worst emotional or mental anguish you've endured?

Year: ---------------------------

February 19

What do you like most about where we live?

Year: ----------------------------------

February 20

What do you worry about?

Year: ---------------------------------

February 21

What's something you screwed up and then tried to hide?

Year: -----------------------------

February 22

What's the scariest /
creepiest place you have
ever been?

Year: ----------------------------

February 23

What do you worry about?

Year: _____

_____

_____

_____

_____

_____

_____

_____

_____

February 24

Do you think the world is
improving or getting worse?
Why?

Year:: -----------------------------

February 25

How do you think society is changing? Do you think we'll change with it?

Year: ----------------------------

February 26

What's the worst thing that
people are proud of?

Year:: ----------------------------

February 27

What's the biggest betrayal
you have ever experienced?

Year:: ----------------------------

February 28

What would be the greatest gift to receive?

Year: -------------------------------

_____

_____

_____

_____

_____

_____

_____

_____

February 29

What is something that you are dreading?

Year: ------------------------------

March 1

What makes you feel super fancy?

Year:: ------------------------------

March 2

What would you want your obituary to say?

Year: ----------------------------

March 3

What has taken up too much of your life?

Year:

March 4

What's the most disheartening and heartening realization you have come to?

Year: : -----------------------------

March 5

What was the hardest lesson
you've had to learn?

Year:: ----------------------------

March 6

Would you take 3 million dollars if it meant that the person you hate most in the world gets 9 million?

Year: ------------------------------

March 7

What part of you as a person
still needs a lot of work?

Year: --------------------------------

March 8

What are some words of wisdom that have stuck with you all these years?

Year: --------------------------

March 9

How well do you know
yourself?

Year: -----------------------

March 10

What is your best (not worst) flaw?

Year: --------------------------

March 11

How forgiving are you?

Year: --------------------------

March 12

Tell me about a time you almost died.

Year: -----------------------------

_____

_____

_____

_____

_____

_____

_____

_____

March 13

Are you ashamed of anything you did in the past? If you are comfortable talking about it, what was it?

Year: ----------------------------

March 14

Do you prefer living in the countryside, in a town, or in a big city? Why?

Year: ------------------------------

March 15

What's your fondest memory
of a tree?

Year: ----------------------

March 16

What are some of the most pleasant sensations for you?

Year:: ----------------------------

March 17

Are you happy with the career path you chose or do you wish you had chosen a different career?

Year:: ---------------------------

March 18

What's the most unethical
thing you do regularly?

Year: ------------------------

March 19

What is way more difficult than it sounds?

Year: -----------------------------

_____

_____

_____

_____

_____

_____

_____

March 20

What job do you think you were born to do?

Year: _____

_____

_____

_____

_____

_____

_____

_____

_____

March 21

What's the biggest financial
mistake you've made?

Year: --------------------------

March 22

What makes you lose faith in humanity when you think about it?

Year: -----------------------------

March 23

What was the most painful thing to hear?

Year: --------------------------

March 24

What biases do you think you have?

Year: ----------------------------

March 25

What are you battling that you don't tell anyone about?

Year: -----------------------------

March 26

What luxury do you enjoy treating yourself to?

Year: _____

_____

_____

_____

_____

_____

_____

_____

_____

March 27

What do you most like to do
when you have alone time?

Year:: ------------------------

March 28

What is normal now that will be considered unethical and barbaric in 100 years?

Year:: -----------------------------

March 29

When you're gone when you want to be remembered for?

Year:: -----------------------------

March 30

If there was a horrible accident and you were unconscious and on life support, how long would you want to be on life support?

Year: -----------------------------

March 31

Do you believe in good luck and bad luck? How about things that are lucky or unlucky?

Year: ------------------------------

---

april 1

Do you believe in good luck and bad luck? How about things that are lucky or unlucky?

Year: --------------------------

----

april 2

If you had a million dollars to give to any charity, what type of charity would you give it to?

Year:: ----------------------------

----

april 3

What's something that a lot of people are afraid of, but you aren't?

Year: ------------------------

----

april 4

If you could open a business
what type of business would
you open?

Year: ----------------------------

----

april 5

What can someone do that makes them immediately unattractive to you, no matter how attractive they are physically?

Year: ------------------------

_____

_____

_____

_____

_____

_____

_____

_____

april 6

What untrue thing did you
believe for an incredibly long
time?

Year: -------------------------

_____

_____

_____

_____

_____

_____

_____

_____

april 7

What were the three most important turning points in your life?

Year: ----------------------------

----

april 8

What animal are you most afraid of?

Year: _____

_____

_____

_____

_____

_____

_____

_____

_____

april 9

What scandal happened in
your neighbor or town when
you were growing up?

Year:: ---------------------------

----

april 10

How well do you think you would handle prison?

Year: ----------------------------------

----

april 11

What's the most awkward social situation you've been in?

Year: -------------------------

_____

_____

_____

_____

_____

_____

_____

_____

april 12

What is something that scares you on a daily basis?

Year: --------------------------

----

april 13

When was the last time you cried?

Year: _____

_____
_____
_____
_____
_____
_____
_____
_____

april 14

What's the most peaceful/restful night of sleep you've had?

Year:: ------------------------------

----

april 15

What's the most dangerous, thrill-seeking thing you would consider doing?

Year:: ----------------------------

----

april 16

What's your biggest regret?

Year:: ----------------------------

april 17

What do you think your best
and worst personality traits
are?

Year: ---------------------------

----

april 18

Who do you miss the most?

Year: ----------------------------

----

april 19

What is the hardest life lesson you've had to learn?

Year: _____

_____

_____

_____

_____

_____

_____

_____

_____

april 20

What do you take for granted?

Year:: ---------------------------

----

april 21

What's the most stressful
situation you've been in? How
did you handle it?

Year:: -------------------------

----

april 22

What's the most ambitious thing you've attempted?

Year: ------------------------------

----

april 23

How often do you change your opinions or how you view the world?

Year: _____

_____

_____

_____

_____

_____

_____

_____

_____

april 24

What's the biggest opportunity you were given?

Year: ----------------------------

----

april 25

What is something we should enjoy more because it won't be around for long?

Year: _____

_____

_____

_____

_____

_____

_____

_____

_____

april 26

What's a question you wish
people would ask more often?

Year: ------------------------------

----

april 27

What is the saddest thing about your life that nobody knows?

Year::

april 28

What are you most
sentimental about?

Year:: ----------------------------

----

april 29

Do you think people more people look down on you or up to you? Why?

Year: ----------------------------

----

april 30

What question do you most want an answer to?

Year: ----------------------------

---

may 1

Do you think people more
people look down on you or up
to you? Why?

Year: --------------------------

----

may 2

What are some of the telltale
signs of a shallow person?

Year: ------------------------

----

may 3

What do you look forward to most in the day?

Year: _____

_____

_____

_____

_____

_____

_____

_____

_____

may 4

If you could instantly learn a talent or skill, what would you want to know how to do?

Year:: -

- -

- -

- -

- -

- -

- -

- -

- -

may 5

When is your favorite time of day?

Year: --------------------------

----

may 6

Do you think people more
people look down on you or up
to you? Why?

Year: ----------------------------

----

may 7

What are the best and worst things about the period of history we are living through?

Year: ----------------------------

----

may 8

What's the most rewarding thing in your daily routine?

Year: _____

_____

_____

_____

_____

_____

_____

_____

_____

may 9

What weird thing stresses you out more than it should?

Year:

may 10

When do you feel like you are really in your element?

Year: ----------------------------

_____

_____

_____

_____

_____

_____

_____

_____

may 11

How likely are you to believe in conspiracy theories?

Year: ------------------------------

may 12

What are some alcohol-induced stories of your younger days?

Year: ----------------------------

----

may 13

What's the best way for someone to improve themselves?

Year::

may 14

What was the most productive time in your life? How about the least productive?

Year: ------------------------------

---

may 15

What three words best describe you?

Year: ---------------------------

----

may 16

What's your secret talent?

Year: ---------------------------

----

may 17

What is your weakness?

Year: _____

may 18

What are two of the most
important events in your life?

Year: ----------------------------

----

may 19

What is something you know is bad for you but you can't seem to get away from it?

Year: _____

_____

_____

_____

_____

_____

_____

_____

_____

may 20

What's the biggest favor you've done for someone?

Year: --------------------------------

----

may 21

How does your current morning routine compare to your ideal morning routine?

Year: ------------------------------

----

may 22

What brings you the most joy?

Year: ---------------------------

----

may 23

What are you purposefully ignoring even though you know you should probably deal with it?

Year: --------------------------------

----

may 24

What do you wish you were better at?

Year: ------------------------------

may 25

Is there anything you did
wrong for years and years,
only to discover later that you
were doing it wrong?

Year: ----------------------------

----

may 26

What is something your parents did or used to do that really embarrassed you?

Year: ---------------------------

----

may 27

What small seemingly insignificant thing did your parents, or someone else say when you were a child that has stuck with you all this time?

Year: ----------------------------

----

may 28

What is the best or worst thing you inherited from your parents?

Year:: ----------------------------

_____

_____

_____

_____

_____

_____

_____

_____

may 29

What made you realize that
your parents were just human
like everyone else?

Year: _____

_____

_____

_____

_____

_____

_____

_____

_____

may 30

What habits do you still have from childhood?

Year: _____

_____

_____

_____

_____

_____

_____

_____

_____

may 31

What family vacations did you take as a child?

Year: ---------------------------

June 1

How traditionally "normal" was
your family?

Year:: ------------------------

June 2

Children are often very similar to their parents. How do you want to be different than your parents? And how do you want to be similar to them?

Year:: ----------------------------

June 3

What school subjects did you like and hate most when you were in school?

Year:: -----------------------------

_____

_____

_____

_____

_____

_____

_____

_____

June 4

What unique game of pretend did you frequently play as a child?

Year: --------------------------

June 5

What movie seriously scarred you as a child or as an adult?

Year: _____

_____

_____

_____

_____

_____

_____

_____

_____

June 6

What irrational fears did you
have as a child?

Year: ------------------------

_____

_____

_____

_____

_____

_____

_____

June 7

What toy played the most significant part in your childhood?

Year:: ------------------------------------

June 8

What are some of your earliest memories?

Year: -------------------------

June 9

What is something I did that
you thought was exceptionally
kind or thoughtful?

Year:: ------------------------------

June 10

What new hobbies or activities would you like to try together as a couple?

Year: ------------------------------

June 11

What's our greatest strength
as a couple?

Year: ----------------------------

June 12

What could we do to make our relationship stronger?

Year: _____

_____

_____

_____

_____

_____

_____

_____

_____

June 13

What is something small that
we can do daily for each other
to make our lives better?

Year::

June 14

How much space / alone time
should people in a relationship
give each other?

Year:: --------------------------

June 15

What questions should partners ask each other before getting married?

Year: -----------------------------

June 16

What do I do that makes you
the happiest?

Year: --------------------------

June 17

How important is it for individuals in a relationship to maintain their own separate identity?

Year: ------------------------------

June 18

What makes our relationship better than other relationships?

Year: --------------------------

June 19

What do you think our life will
look like in 10 years?

Year: ------------------------

June 20

What do you think would bring us closer together as a couple?

Year: ----------------------

June 21

What kind of memories do you
want to make together?

Year:: -------------------------

June 22

What do you think the most essential thing in a successful relationship is?

Year: _____

_____

_____

_____

_____

_____

_____

_____

_____

June 23

What's your favorite way we
spend time together?

Year: ------------------------

_____

_____

_____

_____

_____

_____

_____

_____

June 24

What's your favorite gift I've given you?

Year: --------------------------------

June 25

Where do you want to live
when we retire?

Year: -------------------------

June 26

How well do you think we communicate?

Year: ----------------------------

June 27

What adventure would you like
to go on with me?

Year: ---------------------------

June 28

What's the best relationship
advice you've received?

Year: _____

_____

_____

_____

_____

_____

_____

_____

_____

June 29

What are some things you
really like about me?

Year: -------------------------

June 30

What do you think the hardest thing about marriage/being in a relationship is?

Year: ----------------------------

July 1

What can I do to most help us?

Year:: ------------------------------

July 2

What do you see as your role in our relationship?

Year: _____

_____

_____

_____

_____

_____

_____

_____

_____

July 3

What would be a deal breaker for our relationship, something you couldn't forgive?

Year: -----------------------------

July 4

What makes us different than other couples?

Year: ----------------------------------

July 5

What do you think would be
the best way to strengthen our
relationship?

Year: ------------------------------

July 6

What are some of your relationship goals?

Year: _____

_____

_____

_____

_____

_____

_____

_____

_____

July 7

How realistic do you think couples in movies and TV are?

Year: ------------------------------

July 8

What does a happy and healthy relationship look like to you?

Year: _____

_____

_____

_____

_____

_____

_____

_____

_____

July 9

Do you eventually want to have children? How many children do you eventually want? Why?

Year: -----------------------------

_____

_____

_____

_____

_____

_____

_____

_____

July 10

What's the worst parenting mistake a couple can make?

Year: _____

_____

_____

_____

_____

_____

_____

_____

_____

July 11

What is the best way to raise children?

Year: ----------------------------

July 12

What does a happy and healthy relationship look like to you?

Year: _____

_____

_____

_____

_____

_____

_____

_____

July 13

How would we know if we did
our job as parents well?

Year: _____

_____

_____

_____

_____

_____

_____

_____

_____

July 14

Do you think it is more important for a couple with kids to focus on the kids more or each other more? Why?

Year: ------------------------

July 15

How do you think having kids
will / has changed our lives
and relationship?

Year:: ----------------------------

July 16

What weird food combinations
do you really enjoy?

Year: -----------------------------

_____

_____

_____

_____

_____

_____

_____

_____

July 17

What social stigma does society need to get over?

Year: ------------------------

July 18

What food have you never eaten but would really like to try?

Year: _____

_____
_____
_____
_____
_____
_____
_____
_____

July 19

What's something you really resent paying for?

Year:: ----------------------------

July 20

What would a world populated
by clones of you be like?

Year: ----------------------------

July 21

Do you think that aliens exist?

Year: --------------------------

July 22

What are you currently worried about?

Year: ------------------------------

July 23

Where are some unusual
places you've been?

Year: ----------------------

July 24

Where do you get your news?

Year: -----------------------------

July 25

What are some red flags to watch out for in daily life?

Year: ------------------------

July 26

What movie can you watch over and over without ever getting tired of?

Year: ----------------------------

July 27

When you are old, what do
you think children will ask you
to tell stories about?

Year: --------------------------

July 28

If you could switch two movie characters, what switch would lead to the most inappropriate movies?

Year: ---------------------------------

July 29

What inanimate object would
be the most annoying if it
played loud upbeat music
while being used?

Year: --------------------------

July 30

When did something start out badly for you but in the end, it was great?

Year: _____

_____

_____

_____

_____

_____

_____

_____

_____

July 31

How would your country
change if everyone,
regardless of age, could vote?

Year: --------------------------

August 1

What animal would be cutest if scaled down to the size of a cat?

Year: ----------------------------

August 2

If your job gave you a surprise
three day paid break to rest
and recuperate, what would
you do with those three days?

Year:: ------------------------------

_____

_____

_____

_____

_____

_____

_____

_____

August 3

What's wrong but sounds right?

Year: --------------------------------

_____

_____

_____

_____

_____

_____

_____

_____

August 4

What's the most epic way you've seen someone quit or be fired?

Year: ------------------------------

August 5

If you couldn't be convicted of any one type of crime, what criminal charge would you like to be immune to?

Year: ----------------------------

August 6

What's something that will always be in fashion, no matter how much time passes?

Year: -----------------------------

August 7

What actors or actresses play the same character in almost every movie or show they do?

Year: _____

_____

_____

_____

_____

_____

_____

_____

_____

August 8

What's the best / worst
practical joke that you've
played on someone or that
was played on you?

Year: ----------------------------

August 9

What actors or actresses play the same character in almost every movie or show they do?

Year: _____

_____

_____

_____

_____

_____

_____

_____

_____

August 10

Who do you go out of your way to be nice to?

Year: ----------------------------

August 11

Where do you get most of the decorations for your home?

Year: _____

_____

_____

_____

_____

_____

_____

_____

_____

August 12

What food is delicious but a pain to eat?

Year: ---------------------------

August 13

What "old person" things do you do?

Year: ----------------------------

August 14

What was the last photo you took?

Year: ----------------------------

August 15

Which celebrity do you think is the most down to earth?

Year: ----------------------------

August 16

What would be the worst thing to hear as you are going under anesthesia before heart surgery?

Year: ----------------------------

August 17

What's the spiciest thing you've ever eaten?

Year: _____

_____

_____

_____

_____

_____

_____

_____

_____

August 18

What's the most expensive thing you've broken?

Year: ------------------------------

August 19

What obstacles would be
included in the World's most
amazing obstacle course?

Year: --------------------------

August 20

What makes you roll your eyes every time you hear it?

Year: _____

_____

_____

_____

_____

_____

_____

_____

_____

August 21

What do you think you are much better at than you actually are?

Year: ------------------------------------

August 22

Should kidneys be able to be bought and sold?

Year: --------------------------

August 23

What's the most creative use
of emojis you've ever seen?

Year: _____

_____

_____

_____

_____

_____

_____

_____

_____

August 24

When was the last time you got to tell someone "I told you so."?

Year: -----------------------------

August 25

What riddles do you know?

Year: ------------------------

August 26

What's your cure for hiccups?

Year: --------------------------------

August 27

What invention doesn't get a lot of love, but has greatly improved the world?

Year: _____

_____

_____

_____

_____

_____

_____

_____

_____

August 28

What's the most interesting building you've ever seen or been in?

Year: _____

_____

_____

_____

_____

_____

_____

_____

_____

August 29

What mythical creature do you
wish actually existed?

Year: _____

_____

_____

_____

_____

_____

_____

_____

_____

August 30

What are your most important
rules when going on a date?

Year:: -------------------------

August 31

How do you judge a person?

Year: ------------------------------

September 1

If someone narrated your life, who would you want to be the narrator?

Year: ---------------------------

September 2

How do you judge a person?

Year: _____

_____

_____

_____

_____

_____

_____

_____

_____

September 3

If someone narrated your life, who would you want to be the narrator?

Year: ------------------------------

_____

_____

_____

_____

_____

_____

_____

_____

September 4

What was the most unsettling film you've seen?

Year: _____

_____

_____

_____

_____

_____

_____

_____

_____

September 5

What unethical experiment would have the biggest positive impact on society as a whole?

Year:: ------------------------------

September 6

When was the last time you were snooping, and found something you wish you hadn't?

Year:: -----------------------------

September 7

Which celebrity or band has the worst fan base?

Year: 2024.

Sam Smith.

September 8

What are you interested in that most people aren't?

Year: 2024

Jenny - Flower arranging,
Pastry Making,

September 9

What smartphone feature would you actually be excited for a company to implement?

Year: _____

_____

_____

_____

_____

_____

_____

_____

_____

September 10

What's something people don't worry about but really should?

Year: ------------------------------

September 11

What movie quotes do you
use on a regular basis?

Year:: ---------------------------

September 12

Do you think that children born today will have better or worse lives than their parents?

Year::

September 13

What's the funniest joke you know by heart?

Year: --------------------------

September 14

When was the last time you felt you had a new lease on life?

Year: ------------------------------

September 15

What's the funniest actual name you've heard of someone having?

Year: ------------------------------

September 16

What TV show character would it be the most fun to change places with for a week?

Year: ------------------------

September 17

What was cool when you were young but isn't cool now?

Year: ----------------------------

September 18

If magic was real, what spell
would you try to learn first?

Year: ----------------------------

September 19

If you were a ghost and could possess people, what would you make them do?

Year: -----------------------------

_____

_____

_____

_____

_____

_____

_____

_____

September 20

What goal do you think
humanity is not focused
enough on achieving?

Year: ----------------------------------

September 21

What problem are you currently grappling with?

Year: _____

_____

_____

_____

_____

_____

_____

_____

_____

September 22

What character in a movie could have been great, but the actor they cast didn't fit the role?

Year: ----------------------------

September 23

What game have you spent the most hours playing?

Year:: ------------------------------------

September 24

What's the most comfortable bed or chair you've ever been in?

Year: ------------------------

September 25

What's the craziest conversation you've overheard?

Year: ----------------------------

September 26

What's the hardest you've
ever worked?

Year: ------------------------------

September 27

What's the coldest you've ever been?

Year: --

_____

_____

_____

_____

_____

_____

_____

_____

September 28

Which protagonist from a book
or movie would make the
worst roommate?

Year: ---------------------------

September 29

What's the most ridiculous
thing you have bought?

Year: ------------------------

September 30

What's the funniest comedy
skit you've seen?

Year: --------------------------

October 1

What's the funniest comedy skit you've seen?

Year: -----------------------------

October 2

What's the most depressing meal you've eaten?

Year: _____

_____

_____

_____

_____

_____

_____

_____

_____

October 3

What tips or tricks have you
picked up from your job / jobs?

Year: ----------------------------

_____

_____

_____

_____

_____

_____

_____

_____

October 4

What tips or tricks have you
picked up from your job / jobs?

Year: ------------------------------

October 5

What outdoor activity haven't you tried, but would like to?

Year: --------------------------

October 6

What songs hit you with a
wave of nostalgia every time
you hear them?

Year:: --------------------------

October 7

What's the worst backhanded compliment you could give someone?

Year: ---------------------------

October 8

What's the most interesting documentary you've ever watched?

Year: --------------------------------

October 9

What was the last song you
sang along to?

Year: ------------------------------

_____

_____

_____

_____

_____

_____

_____

_____

October 10

What's the funniest thing you've done or had happen while your mind was wandering?

Year: -----------------------------

October 11

What app can you not believe
someone hasn't made yet?

Year: ------------------------------

October 12

When was the last time you
face palmed?

Year::: -----------------------------

October 13

If you were given five million dollars to open a small museum, what kind of museum would you create?

Year: ------------------------------

October 14

Which of your vices or bad habits would be the hardest to give up?

Year: ----------------------------

October 15

What really needs to be modernized?

Year: ----------------------------

October 16

When was the last time you slept more than nine hours?

Year: ------------------------------

October 17

How comfortable are you speaking in front of large groups of people?

Year: ------------------------------

October 18

What's your worst example of procrastination?

Year: ------------------------------

October 19

Who has zero filter between
their brain and mouth?

Year: ------------------------

_____

_____

_____

_____

_____

_____

_____

_____

October 20

What was your most recent lie?

Year: --

October 21

When was the last time you
immediately regretted
something you said?

Year: -----------------------------

October 22

What would be the best thing
you could reasonably expect
to find in a cave?

Year:: -------------------------

October 23

What did you think was going
to be amazing but turned out
to be horrible?

Year: ----------------------

October 24

What bit of trivia do you know
that is very interesting but also
very useless?

Year: ------------------------------

October 25

What's the silliest thing you've seen someone get upset about?

Year: ----------------------------

October 26

What animal or plant do you
think should be renamed?

Year:

October 27

What was the best thing that happened to you today?

Year: ------------------------------

October 28

What's the most boring super hero you can come up with?

Year: ------------------------

October 29

What would be some of the downsides of certain superpowers?

Year: --------------------------------

_____

_____

_____

_____

_____

_____

_____

_____

October 30

What word is a lot of fun to say?

Year:: --------------------------

October 31

What current trend do you hope will go on for a long time?

Year: -------------------------

November 1

Where's your go to restaurant
for amazing food?

Year: _____

_____

_____

_____

_____

_____

_____

_____

_____

November 2

What's something that all your friends agree on?

Year: -----------------------------

November 3

What's your best story from a wedding?

Year: _____

_____

_____

_____

_____

_____

_____

_____

_____

November 4

What languages do you wish
you could speak?

Year: ----------------------------

November 5

What's the most pleasant
sounding accent?

Year: -------------------------------

November 6

What country is the strangest?

Year: --------------------------------

November 7

What's the funniest word in the English language?

Year: ----------------------------

November 8

What's some insider
knowledge that only people in
your line of work have?

Year: ----------------------------

November 9

What current trend do you hope will go on for a long time?

Year: -------------------------

November 10

Who do you wish you could
get back into contact with?

Year: ------------------------

November 11

How do you make yourself
sleep when you can't seem to
get to sleep?

Year:: -----------------------

November 12

What are some of the best vacations you've had?

Year:: -----------------------------

November 13

What's the craziest video
you've ever seen?

Year: -------------------------------

November 14

What's your "Back in my day, we…"?

Year: _____

_____

_____

_____

_____

_____

_____

_____

_____

November 15

What animal would be the most terrifying if it could speak?

Year: _____

_____

_____

_____

_____

_____

_____

_____

_____

November 16

What's the worst hairstyle you've ever had?

Year: ----------------------------

November 17

What habit do you have now
that you wish you started
much earlier?

Year: --------------------------

November 18

What about the opposite sex confuses you the most?

Year: ----------------------------

November 19

When was the last time you yelled at someone?

Year: ------------------------------

November 20

What's the opposite of a koala?

Year: ------------------------------

_____

_____

_____

_____

_____

_____

_____

_____

November 21

What kinds of things do you like to cook or are good at cooking?

Year: _____

_____

_____

_____

_____

_____

_____

_____

_____

November 22

What life skills are rarely taught but extremely useful?

Year: ----------------------------

November 23

What movie universe would be the worst to live out your life in?

Year: ------------------------------

November 24

What kinds of things do you like to cook or are good at cooking?

Year:: -----------------------

November 25

What's the most ridiculous animal on the planet?

Year: _____

_____

_____

_____

_____

_____

_____

_____

_____

November 26

What's the worst thing you've eaten out of politeness?

Year: ------------------------------

November 27

What's the most historic thing that has happened in your lifetime?

Year: --------------------------

November 28

What has been blown way out
of proportion?

Year:: ----------------------------

November 29

What has been blown way out
of proportion?

Year: ------------------------------

November 30

When was a time you acted nonchalant but were going crazy inside?

Year: ----------------------------

December 1

What's about to get much better?

Year: _____

_____

_____

_____

_____

_____

_____

_____

_____

December 2

What are some clever examples of misdirection you've seen?

Year: ------------------------------

_____

_____

_____

_____

_____

_____

_____

_____

December 3

What's your funniest story involving a car?

Year: ------------------------------

December 4

What would be the click-bait
titles of some popular movies?

Year: -----------------------

December 5

What would your perfect bar
look like?

Year: ---------------------------

_____

_____

_____

_____

_____

_____

_____

_____

December 6

What's the scariest non-horror movie?

Year:: ------------------------------

December 7

What's the most amazing true
story you've heard?

Year: ----------------------------

December 8

What's the grossest food that
you just can't get enough of?

Year: _____

_____
_____
_____
_____
_____
_____
_____
_____

December 9

What brand are you most loyal to?

Year: --------------------------

December 10

What's the most awkward
thing that happens to you on a
regular basis?

Year: --------------------------

December 11

What movie or book do you
know the most quotes from?

Year: -----------------------------

December 12

What was one of the most interesting concerts you've been to?

Year: ----------------------------

December 13

Where are you not welcome anymore?

Year: ------------------------

_____

_____

_____

_____

_____

_____

_____

_____

December 14

What do you think could be done to improve the media?

Year: ---------------------------------

December 15

What's the most recent show
you've binge watched?

Year: -

- -

- -

- -

- -

- -

- -

- -

- -

December 16

What's the worst movie trope?

Year: ----------------------------

December 17

What's a common experience
for many people that you've
never experienced?

Year: ------------------------

December 18

What's the smartest thing
you've seen an animal do?

Year: ------------------------------

_____

_____

_____

_____

_____

_____

_____

_____

December 19

What's the most annoying noise?

Year: _____

December 20

What's your haunted house story?

Year: _____

_____

_____

_____

_____

_____

_____

_____

_____

_____

December 21

What's the scariest non-horror movie?

Year: ----------------------------

December 22

What's the saddest scene in a
movie or TV series?

Year: ---------------------------

December 23

What's the most frustrating product you own?

Year: _____

_____

_____

_____

_____

_____

_____

_____

_____

December 24

What inconsequential super power would you like to have?

Year: -

- -

- -

- -

- -

- -

- -

- -

- -

- -

December 25

What qualities do all your friends have in common?

Year: ------------------------------

December 26

What odd smell do you really enjoy?

Year: ----------------------------------

December 27

What odd smell do you really enjoy?

Year:: ----------------------------

December 28

What's the best lesson you've learned from a work of fiction?

Year: --------------------------------

December 29

What food do you crave most often?

Year:

December 30

Who in your life has the best / worst luck?

Year: ------------------------------

December 31

Which apocalyptic dystopia do
you think is most likely?

Year: _____

_____

_____

_____

_____

_____

_____

_____

_____

—